NOAH

A Journal of Praise

NOAH

A Journal of Praise

Written by NANCY E. GANZ

Illustrated by MATTHEW SAMPLE II

Shepherd Press

Noah: A Journal of Praise
© 2015 by Nancy E. Ganz
Illustrated by Matthew Sample II

Paper ISBN: 978-1-63342-110-3
ePub ISBN: 978-1-63342-111-0
Mobi ISBN: 978-1-63342-112-7

Published by Shepherd Press
P.O. Box 24
Wapwallopen, Pennsylvania 18660

Typesetting by Matthew Sample II
Cover Design by Tobias Outerwear for Books

_____

First Printing, 2015
Printed in the United States of America

NALC9NIVRI

PAH 22 21 20 19 18 17 16 15
14 13 12 11 10 9 8 7 6 5 4 3 2 1

eBooks: www.shepherdpress.com/ebooks

Foreword

When people go on a journey, they often keep a journal. Noah went on an amazing journey. Did he take scrolls with him on which to write everything? We do not know. We will have to wait until heaven to hear Noah tell the story of his voyage. Of course, Noah and his sons told their children and grandchildren and great-grandchildren about the flood, and the story was passed on from generation to generation.

You would think there would be a whole book in the Bible called the "Book of Noah," but the account of that incredible journey is recorded in only one small section of the book of Genesis. As we read that account we can imagine what it was like for Noah. Had he kept a journal, I think we would have found that it was a "Journal of Praise." Let's pretend that we are reading some pages from Noah's journal.

Notes
1. The full account of the flood is found in Genesis 6:5–8:22.
2. A.N. = Anno Noah (Age of Noah) because the dates are based on Noah's years.

My family and I moved into the ark a week ago, as God commanded, but today is the seventh day.

Early this morning we walked up the ramp of the ark for the very last time. All week animals have been coming to us, but today I was filled with a feeling of grief and awe and dread, as the last two tiny creatures climbed aboard, for I knew that the end was very near, that the day of destruction was upon us. Yes, today is the seventh day, the day God promised that he would destroy the earth and every living creature upon it. I believed God's word.

Outside the whole wonderful world was teeming with life of every kind. There was a whole world of people too, still refusing to believe that God, who has endured their wickedness for so long, would delay no longer.

I was thankful that our God himself shut the door of the ark. Would I have had the strength to do it? How thankful I am that the opening and shutting of doors in heaven and on earth are in the hands of my mighty and merciful Master!

I am thankful that we cannot see the dreadful destruction that is taking place. God is doing all that he promised, but who could imagine how terrifying that would be?

Even now, as I write, the ark shakes violently with the earthquakes. And the rain—it is not pattering or even pounding against the roof of the ark, as I imagined. No, there is a steady roaring noise. When it first began, it seemed as if the roof would collapse upon us. The noise of the deluge is deafening, terrifying. It is difficult, even in this place of safety, not to panic.

I realize now, even here in the ark, even here in this shelter of God, that we must live by faith. We must entrust our lives to God and not be afraid.

Sometimes, beyond the roar of the rain, I think I hear the bellowing of animals and the screaming of people.

Lord, I thank you for saving us.

18/02/600 A.N.

We have survived the first day of the flood.

We see nothing beyond the walls of the ark. We hear nothing beyond the roar of the rain. The ark continues to rattle as the LORD rips apart the earth.

No one slept last night. We spent the hours of darkness on our knees, praying to the LORD to spare us. Daylight, which was also dark, brought no relief.

I wonder: How long will it take God to destroy the world? How long will his anger pour down? He told me: "Forty days and forty nights."

I cannot imagine the terror of this destruction continuing for so long, for even another day. How will we be able to endure it?

We must live by faith. We must not be overwhelmed by fear.

Lord, I thank you for giving me,
and all those with me in the ark,
another day of life.

An amazing thing happened today. The ark jolted violently and then began to float. For so many years the ark has stood still on dry ground. It always seemed more like a barn than a boat. But now it is floating.

It seems strange that there is water here, deep water covering my home, my fields, the roads where I walked, the towns where I preached. It is all underwater. Where I once lived no longer exists. It has all vanished from the face of the earth.

The ark is my only home now.

God is my only refuge.

I am drifting over the earth now, but I am firmly rooted in my God.

Lord, thank you for this new home,
that floats safely above the waters of destruction.

Floating on these wild waters has brought a new fear, the fear of being dashed to pieces on the rocks.

We do not know where we are going. We cannot see where we are going. These waters are all unknown. There are no harbors, no havens. We can neither anchor our ship nor steer it. The ark has neither sails nor oars. What can we do? The ark is completely out of our control.

Perhaps for that we should be thankful, for we can only entrust our lives to God. We must do so daily, hourly. We must combat our fear with faith. As we float in the ark, we must rest in God.

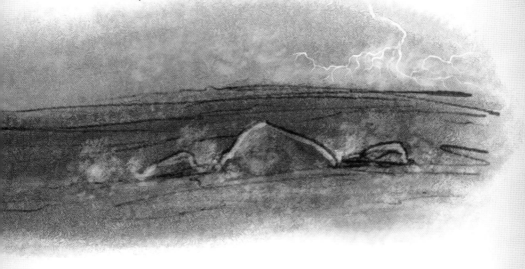

Lord, we thank you that day after day
in these raging waters
you steer the ark safely away from the rocks,
for these waters are not unknown to you.

17/03/600 A.N.

We have been shut in the ark for one full month. The roaring of the rain continues.

We have not grown used to the noise. Even when we sleep, we hear it driving into our dreams.

How strange it is that many of the animals have fallen into a deep sleep. They do not awake, even to eat, yet they are alive.

Lord, we give you thanks.
The one who watches Noah and his ark
never slumbers, nor sleeps.
Your eyes are always upon us.

27/03/600 A.N.

Forty days have passed since the beginning of the flood.

Today marked a definite change in the intensity of the rain. By evening the drops drumming on the roof of the ark sounded like a normal rainstorm.

We could actually talk without having to shout. When we prayed to the LORD together, we could hear each other's prayers. When we sang praises to our God, we could hear the music of our voices. Some of our pet songbirds joined in the chorus. How wonderful to our ears was that time of worship!

We all rejoiced that the roar of the rain had subsided, that the sounds of life were no longer drowned in the deafening roar of destruction. Blessed be the name of our God!

> Lord, we thank you for the sounds
> that we heard this night—
> the sounds of your praises. Your anger is ending.
> We give you thanks
> that your work of destroying the world
> is almost complete.

28/03/600 A.N.

The forty days and forty nights are finished. Just as God promised, the rain has ceased. There is peace on the earth. Not even a drop of rain ripples the water's surface.

Outside the ark all is quiet. There is not one sound, not one whisper, not one breath . . . from any creature. They are all gone.

God said, "Every creature that has the breath of life in it, everything on earth, will perish." It is finished, according to the word of the LORD.

The silence is overwhelming. The stillness in this new world is awesome.

Inside the ark, I listen. I hear only a few sounds; a cricket chirping in the corner of my room, a dog barking somewhere on a lower deck, people talking quietly in the loft above me. Except in this place, in the ark, the sounds of life have ceased upon the earth.

In heaven the angels glorify God, but here on earth, there is only one place left where one can hear the sounds of God's praises. It is here in the ark.

We have a great responsibility to praise our God continually.

O Lord, I will exalt you,
for you have lifted me . . .
above death,
above its silence,
above the grave,
which is now the whole world.
May these lips ever praise your holy name.

A new question plagues me. Since water now covers the entire earth, where will it go? How will God get rid of it?

In a normal rainstorm, the water soaks into earth or it runs into streams and lakes and seas—but this time, there is nowhere for the water to go.

The whole world is one enormous ocean. How can so much water ever disappear? Even the tops of the highest mountains are covered by it. Will the sun dry it up? That would take years . . . no, centuries!

We could all starve to death in the ark. Will this ark become a huge floating coffin for the last creatures that live upon the earth?

Lord, forgive me for such questions.
You have saved us from the waters of the flood—
and you will continue to save us from them.
I offer you my humble and fearful praise.

Dreadful doubts continue to disturb me: Has God forgotten us?

The whole world is silent—and so is God. He has not spoken to us since the day he said, "Go into the ark."

I must have faith in my God. I must believe his word, spoken to me so long ago. I must trust in his promise.

He said, "Everything on earth will perish, but I will establish my covenant with you."

Lord, I thank you
that you are a covenant-keeping God.
What you have promised, I know you will fulfill.
Thank you for your word,
which gives me hope, when all appears hopeless.

Confirm my faith.
I believe you, Lord,
but help my unbelief.

14/04/600 A.N.

We were awakened in the night by a new sound—a wind, one that was blowing hard.

We wonder: Will it become a horrible, howling hurricane?

The ark has been tossing terribly upon the waves, but what is worse is the turmoil in our hearts.

We wonder: Is this another storm? Will there

be more rain? Isn't the flood over yet? Is God angry again? How long will the LORD's wrath rage against this world?

We fear that the flood will go on forever and ever.

Lord, we know not what you are doing.
Your ways are not our ways.
We can only trust you.
We thank you that you are a merciful God,
as well as the almighty God.
We entrust ourselves to your love.

You alone are our help and our savior.
O Lord, do not delay.

21/04/600 A.N.

All week the wind has continued, but there has been no rain. A realization has come to me: This is how the LORD is going to dry the earth—with a wind.

God has not forgotten us. Let us shout this news over the waters of the whole world: "God has remembered Noah and all the wild animals that were with him in the ark. Hallelujah! God has sent a wind over the earth to take away the waters. Even the wind and the waves obey him!"

What was for us last week "a horrible, howling hurricane" has become a wonderful, whistling wind. It is music for our ears and reassurance for our hearts because we know that the floodwaters are receding.

We know that God has not forgotten us.

Lord, we thank you for the wind.
We thank you for remembering us and loving us.
We thank you for this ark,
which rocks upon the waves like a giant cradle,
giving your creatures peace.

We thank you for your loving hands,
which safely hold us
and gently rock us to sleep.

The voyage is longer than any of us ever imagined possible. How vast is this world!

We sail on and on and on . . . never sighting land, never coming to the edge, never reaching the end. We never arrive at that place where the water and the sky meet.

O Lord, creator of the heavens and the earth,
how great you are!
How awesome are your deeds!
How mighty are your works!

Today is the seventeenth day of the seventh month. We have been locked in the ark for one hundred and fifty days.

Most of that time we have been either gently rocking or wildly pitching. Since we have been upon the water there has been constant motion, but today it stopped.

The ark is still. It is a strange sensation and we find it difficult to walk, having developed "sea legs" over these five months. Why have we stopped moving?

I think the explanation is this: The ark has become stuck on a mountain, one that is beneath the water, because we still can see no land. We did not crash into the side of this underwater mountain; no, the ark just softly and safely came to rest upon it.

It showed us—again—that God is in control of everything, both great and small. It was his mighty hand which destroyed the world completely; it was his gentle hand which landed our boat easily.

Nothing is left to chance in this universe. There is no such thing as "chance." It is a figment of man's warped imagination.

Lord, we thank you
for the safe landing of the ark.
We thank you that the ark has come to rest

after its long dangerous voyage.
We thank you for stilling the ark . . . and us.
Our hearts have also been turbulent,
tossed upon waves of doubt.

Forgive us. O Lord, who commands the universe,
we thank you for noticing us,
for seeing one small boat upon this vast ocean,
and for causing it to obey you also.
O Lord, we thank you for loving us!

17/09/600 A.N.
We have been at rest for two full months, but still there is no visible sign of land anywhere.

However, we know that the water is being dried up by the wind, which has continued to blow steadily.

We know this because the water-level mark on the side of the ark goes down. Since we have been stuck upon this mountain, we have been able to measure the receding waters in this way.

Lord, grant us patience.
We thank you for
the small encouragements you give us each day.
We thank you for the great encouragement
of your word,
in which we hope.

Today is a day to remember, a day to celebrate, a day to praise our God.

It is the first day of the tenth month—and on this date we sighted land. It is the first day we have seen the earth, since the LORD flooded the world. We can see the rocks of the mountains upon which the ark is resting.

Hurrah! Hurrah! The tops of the mountains are visible.

Never have rocks seemed so beautiful to me. I long to stand upon them, to feel the solid earth beneath my feet again.

Lord, I thank you
that your anger lasts but a moment,
your grace—a whole lifetime!
I thank you that
you did not destroy the earth
forever in your wrath,
but only for a season . . .
and now you are creating it again.
You are unveiling it
before my eyes.

Day by day
I will gaze upon your wonderful work.
Day by day
I will praise you for your mercy,
which endures forever.

Every day God changes the shape of the earth.

The "islands" of rock continually grow. I watch the little "shoreline" here changing, constantly changing, as new land emerges from out of the depths. I am watching with fascination a fragment of the recreation of the world.

Daily, my eyes behold the wonders of God.

Lord, your mercies are new every morning.
I thank you.

Forty days have passed since we first sighted land.

Today I opened the window and set free the first creature from the ark.

To whom was this honor given? I did not give it to the prettiest of my pets.

No, I bestowed this honor upon a plain old raven, a scavenger. I knew that he would survive, finding something to eat among the bits of flesh that must be floating outside the ark. A seed-eating bird might find no food. That was the reason I released a raven. I set free my big black bird to be my spy.

He was so happy to spread his wings again. He soared around and around the ark, cawing with delight and calling to his mate to join him.

After some time he flew away over the waters, searching for a meal—glad to be hunting on his own,

glad to be providing for himself.

My family and I had great pleasure watching the first of the birds fly away from the ark. I was surprised that a raven, a plain old raven, could bring tears of joy to my eyes.

He was so magnificent as he soared through the air with his new-found freedom. Nor was he about to give up that freedom. He flew back and forth from the ark throughout the day, but he would not come to the window where I could catch him and cage him again. No, he is enjoying his life out in the world.

He perches proudly upon the ark, avoiding the window. He hops upon the nearby rocks to show us that he is the first to walk upon the land.

Then he flies away again . . . just for the sheer joy of flying! I expect we will hear him cawing his praises around the ark all through the night.

Lord, we thank you
for the lowliest of your creatures
and for the joy they give us.
We thank you
that the exodus from the ark
has begun today
and for the hope which fills our hearts
because of it.

One day, we too will leave the ark
and walk upon the earth again.
Thank you, Lord.

17/11/600 A.N.

A week has passed since I set free the raven. He is
doing well and continues to fly back and forth from
the ark, impatient for the release of his mate. He will
have to wait awhile.

Today I set free a dove, a soft white dove. I
wondered: Would such a bird be able to survive
out in the world? Would she be able to find a nesting
place? a feeding ground?

My answer came this evening: She returned to
the ark because the earth was not ready for her
yet. She still needed the shelter and supplies of
the ark. The earth could not yet provide these
things for her.

Gentle little creature—she flew to me by the
window and alighted upon my outstretched arm,
cooing softly, pleadingly, to be allowed back into
the ark. I know now that it is not safe yet to leave our
refuge. We must all remain in the ark awhile longer.

Lord, thank you for the information
that we received today.
Help us to be patient.
Help us to wait until the right time
to leave the ark.
Thank you for this shelter
you have provided for us all.

24/11/600 A.N.
Another week has passed.

Again I sent the dove from the ark. Again she returned, but this time she brought me a present. In her beak she carried a freshly plucked olive leaf!

We have all kinds of dried plants upon the ark to feed the animals—but nothing green, nothing fresh. To see a single fresh green leaf was a real gift for my water-weary eyes.

The information my little spy brought me was good too. Although the earth is not ready yet for my little dove, trees are beginning to grow again. This is wonderful news.

Now I know that the water is truly receding. There is now earth again, in which the plants can grow.

Lord, we thank you
that you are causing
the earth to be clothed
with green
and covered with plants
once again.

Another seven days has passed.

I sent out my little dove one more time, but from this trip she did not return to me. She has found a place to build her nest. The earth, not the ark, is her home once again.

Brave little bird—I wonder if she is lonely out there, since she is the only creature dwelling on the earth. Even my scavenger friend, the raven, keeps the ark's roof as his headquarters.

It is an important day. The first of the ark's creatures has left "home" to settle in the new world.

It will not be long, I pray, until we can all leave here, to live once more upon our beloved earth.

Lord, watch over the little dove,
who is all alone in the world.
We thank you for being
a God who cares for even the smallest birds.
Since you love them, Lord,
we know that you love us too.

We thank you for your great love.
We ask, O Lord,
that soon we too may return to the earth,
which your hands have remade for us.

Lord, I have neglected to thank you for this,
but I do so now. Thank you for the flood,
which has washed away the wicked,
which has scoured the evil off the face of the earth.
We long to live in this new, clean,
unpolluted, undefiled world.

01/01/601 A.N.

Today is my birthday. I am six hundred and one years old. I have lived through the destruction of the world. My eyes have seen many things over these many centuries, but today I beheld a most wondrous sight.

Today my sons and I removed the covering of the ark. The roof, which has sheltered us for so long, was lifted off today to celebrate my birthday. It was wonderful to see the sky again, the whole expanse of the heavens, and to stand in the sunshine and to breathe the fresh air.

What could be a more wonderful gift on my birthday? But there was something more wonderful.

Wonder of wonders—today I gazed over the earth and I saw that the ground was dry!

At times I had despaired that I would ever see land again, but there it was.

I slowly turned and in all directions, for miles and miles and miles . . . there was land, dry land. The ark is resting high upon a mountain, so the view from here is magnificent.

How beautiful is this new world that God has made for my eyes to see!

My family was anxious to set out immediately, just to explore, but something or Someone, restrains me. We will wait. To see the land is enough for today.

Lord, I thank you for giving me
601 years of life—
and that you granted me life
during a time
when you destroyed all life.

Lord, I thank you for allowing
my old eyes to see the earth again.
I thank you that the ark's roof,
which has sheltered us for so long,
was removed today, my birthday.

Tonight, as I view the heavens,
which you have adorned
with countless twinkling gems,
I know that truly you are the Lord of love!

17/02/601 A.N.

More than a month has passed since my birthday, but today is another special day, an anniversary. One year ago, on this very day, the flood began. We have been shut in the ark for one full year.

Again my family wanted to go into the world. "Surely this is the day to leave the ark," they said.

But I replied, "No. We entered at God's command; we will also leave at God's command."

And so we wait for the word of the LORD.

Lord, we thank you for this year of the flood,
in which you have preserved our lives.

27/02/601 A.N.

Today was an exciting day, for the LORD spoke to me again.

God has been silent for over a year, but today he spoke to me these blessed words "Come out." God said, "Come out of the ark, you and your wife and your sons and their wives. Bring out every kind of living creature that is with you . . . so they can multiply on the earth and be fruitful and increase in number upon it."

It was a marvelous day! We watched the birds fly away in pairs, singing with joy because they were soaring into the sky again. We watched the wild animals descend, two by two, down the side of the mountain.

Already some of them are just dots in the distance; many others are already out of sight. It is sad to think we may never see these magnificent creatures again.

Other animals—such as the cows, sheep, goats, chickens, horses, rabbits, and maybe the monkeys—we are keeping with us as stock or pets.

My family is outside, ready to go, ready to begin our climb down the mountain.

This is the last time I will write in my journal of praise. Our life in the ark has come to an end. Now we will begin a new life in a new world. I want to conclude my journal with these words: Praise the Lord!

Give thanks to the Lord, for he is good;
his love endures forever.
Who can proclaim the mighty acts of the Lord
or fully declare his praise?
No one can give God the glory due his name,
yet he is pleased to accept
our lowly offerings of praise.

Praise the Lord!

"Never again will I curse the ground because of man, even though every inclination of his heart is evil from childhood. And never again will I destroy all living creatures, as I have done.

"As long as the earth endures,
seedtime and harvest,
cold and heat,
summer and winter,
day and night
will never cease."

Genesis 8:21–22

Noah's Sketches

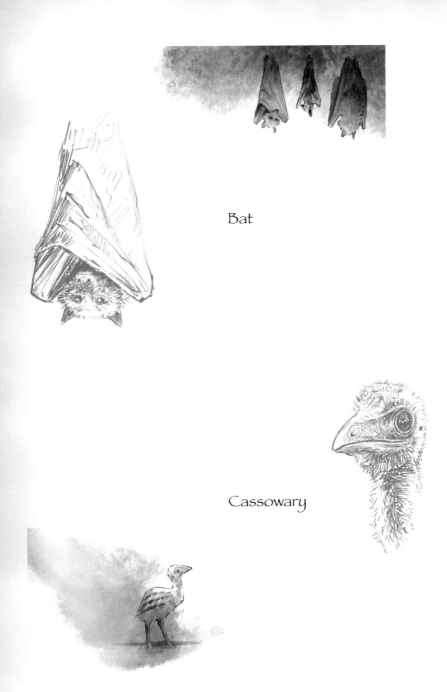

Bat

Cassowary

Chevrotain

Civet

Cuscus

Dodo

Gerenuk

Hoatzin

Hedgehog

Honey Badger

Iguana

Microraptor

Owl

Pangolin

Platypus

Psittacosaurus

Salamander

Slow Loris

Snail

Tapir

Toad

Turtle

Wombat